DRONES ARE EVERYWHERE!

DRONES FOR HELPING THE ENVIRONMENT

SHANNON HARTS

PowerKiDS press.
New York

Published in 2020 by The Rosen Publishing Group, Inc.
29 East 21st Street, New York, NY 10010

First Edition

Editor: Shannon Harts
Book Design: Tanya Dellaccio

Photo Credits: Cover (background) Dmytro Balkhovitin/Shutterstock.com; cover (drone) Suwin/Shutterstock.com; series background Djem/Shuttertock.com; p. 5 Travlerpix/Shutterstock.com; p. 7 Mr. kitsadakron Pongha/EyeEm/Getty Images; p. 9 (both) PIERRE ANDRIEU/AFP/Getty Images; p. 11 Rich Carey/Shutterstock.com; p. 13 Alexander Kolomietz/Shutterstock.com; p. 15 (main) Love Silhouette/Shutterstock.com; p. 15 (inset) NASA/Getty Images News/Getty Images; p. 17 Nolanberg 11/Shutterstock.com; p. 19 BORIS HORVAT/AFP/Getty Images; p. 21 kckate16/Shutterstock.com; p. 22 LaineN/Shutterstock.com.

Library of Congress Cataloging-in-Publication Data

Names: Harts, Shannon.
Title: Drones for helping the environment / Shannon Harts.
Description: New York : PowerKids Press, 2020. | Series: Drones are everywhere! | Includes glossary and index.
Identifiers: ISBN 9781725309227 (pbk.) | ISBN 9781725309241 (library bound) | ISBN 9781725309234 (6 pack)
Subjects: LCSH: Environmental protection–Technological innovations–Juvenile literature. | Earth sciences–Remote sensing–Juvenile literature. | Drone aircraft in remote sensing–Juvenile literature.

Classification: LCC TD170.15 H36 2020 | DDC 363.7–dc23

Manufactured in the United States of America
CPSIA Compliance Information: Batch #CWPK20. For Further Information contact Rosen Publishing, New York, New York at 1-800-237-9932.

CONTENTS

JUST TAKING OFF 4
MORE TREES, PLEASE! 6
FIGHTING FOREST FIRES—FAST! . 8
WONDROUS WILDLIFE PROTECTORS 10
GETTING INTO ICY SITUATIONS! . . 12
RENEWABLE ENERGY HELPERS . . . 14
OLD MACDONALD HAD A ...DRONE? 16
DRONE DELIVERY! 18
STAYING SAFE UP THERE 20
TAKING GREEN TO NEW HEIGHTS 22
GLOSSARY 23
INDEX 24
WEBSITES 24

JUST TAKING OFF

If you've seen a robot with spinning metal blades humming high in the sky, you've likely seen a drone. Drones are small aircraft that can fly without someone onboard. Instead, a person flies a drone from the ground using a **remote control**. The growing number of uses for drones includes helping the **environment**.

From saving wildlife to planting trees and stopping forest fires, there are many ways drones can help the planet. However, there are also problems to address, such as safety concerns.

DRONE DETAILS

DRONES ARE HERE TO STAY! THE FEDERAL AVIATION ADMINISTRATION (FAA) BELIEVES THAT IN 2020, AS MANY AS 7 MILLION DRONES WILL HAVE BEEN SOLD IN THE UNITED STATES!

Special drones can fly over areas to make sure there isn't too much air pollution.

MORE TREES, PLEASE!

Even though they don't have hands, some drones can plant trees much faster than people! A company called BioCarbon Engineering has made drones that can plant as many as 120 trees per minute. Two people can control 10 drones that shoot 400,000 seedpods a day from 10 feet (3 m) in the air.

Trees play an important part in cleaning the air we breathe. They also lessen the effects of climate change, or the long-term changes in Earth's average weather conditions.

DRONE DETAILS

BIOCARBON ENGINEERING DRONES FIRE SEEDPODS INTO THE GROUND AT A RATE OF ABOUT TWO PER SECOND. THE COMPANY AIMS TO PLANT ABOUT 500 BILLION TREES BY 2060!

In the nation of Myanmar, BioCarbon Engineering drones are planting coastal trees—called mangroves—to help keep people safe during powerful storms called cyclones.

FIGHTING FOREST FIRES—FAST!

There's a growing problem in the western United States: climate change is making forest fires bigger. Since 1984, the additional area burned yearly has grown larger than the state of Maryland! However, drones can help spot small fires before they grow out of control.

In 2017, a system called Fuego would use drones equipped with special **infrared** cameras to find fires in their early stages. This alerts firefighters so they can fight forest fires sooner.

DRONE DETAILS

FUEGO, LED BY UC BERKELEY **ASTROPHYSICIST** CARLTON PENNYPACKER, WOULD ALSO INCLUDE **SATELLITES** AND PLANES FLOWN BY PEOPLE. IT COULD SCAN THE ENTIRE WESTERN UNITED STATES ABOUT EVERY THREE MINUTES LOOKING FOR NEW BIG FIRES.

A drone, also called an unmanned aerial vehicle, took this image of a forest fire in 2012 in southwestern France. The French company Fly-n-Sense (FNS) tested drones to spot forest fires from above.

WONDROUS WILDLIFE PROTECTORS

There are many ways drones can help save Earth's wonderful wildlife. Drones helped save pilot whales from hunters in 2014. A group called the Sea Shepherd Conservation Society led the effort.

Drones were used to spot pilot whales when they got too close to the Faroe Islands in the North Atlantic Ocean, where they're hunted, and then small boats would be sent out to scare the whales away. The method worked! From June to September 2013, about 1,300 whales were killed. In 2014, with the drones' help, only 32 were killed.

DRONE DETAILS

AN UNDERWATER DRONE WITH FIVE CAMERAS HAS BEEN USED TO OBSERVE GREAT WHITE SHARKS. IT SHOWED A LOT OF NEW FACTS ABOUT HOW THESE TOP PREDATORS HUNT IN DEEP WATER. THE SHARKS ACTUALLY BIT THE DRONE AT ONE POINT!

In Kenya, drones have helped reduce poaching, or the illegal hunting, of wildlife by up to 96 percent!

GETTING INTO ICY SITUATIONS!

Climate change is causing Arctic ice to melt, resulting in sea level rise that puts coastal regions around the world in danger. In 2015, a scientist named Christopher Zappa started working to use drones with cameras that can sense heat to observe melting ice in the Arctic. Drones can fit in more places than manned aircraft.

Special drones were made to study marginal ice zones, or areas where ocean waves affect seasonal ice. Using infrared cameras, the drones can collect data, or facts, on ice changes.

DRONE DETAILS

DRONES CAN TAKE PICTURES FROM THE AIR TO HELP PEOPLE FIND WAYS OF PROTECTING, OR SAVING, COASTS. ONE AREA THAT IS BEING STUDIED IS LOUISIANA'S BARRIER ISLANDS THAT LIMIT **STORM SURGE**.

Drones can help people understand how fast glaciers are melting by finding things such as ponds of meltwater and cliffs that don't have as much ice.

RENEWABLE ENERGY HELPERS

You've probably seen at least one giant white **wind turbine** spinning way up in the sky, but do you ever wonder how someone might be able to make sure all the parts up there are working? That's where drones come in!

Drones with special cameras can fly up and take pictures of the turbine parts to help find any issues. Wind turbines are important because they create a type of renewable energy, or power that can be renewed by natural systems.

DRONE DETAILS

DRONES WITH SPECIAL CAMERAS CAN CAPTURE THERMAL IMAGES, OR PICTURES THAT SHOW AN OBJECT'S HEAT, TO MEASURE HOW WELL **SOLAR PANELS** ARE WORKING. SOME CAN BE CONTROLLED BY JUST A FEW TAPS ON A SMARTPHONE!

The company AeroVironment created a solar-powered drone (above right) in 1999, that NASA scientists hope will help them understand how to fly on Mars!

OLD MACDONALD HAD A ... DRONE?

Weird weather from climate change is making it even harder to be a farmer, but drones can help. In places with major droughts, or long periods of dry weather, drones are saving water by finding holes in systems that water crops.

Drones can also help farmers use less water and **fertilizer**. Thermal cameras attached to drones can find areas where crops need water most and where it's not needed. By creating satellite maps, drones can also help farmers make smarter decisions about using fertilizer, which can cause waterway pollution.

Some drones can cover about 1,000 acres (404 ha) in a single flight!

DRONE DETAILS

AGRICULTURE, OR THE SCIENCES AND PRACTICES OF FARMING, COULD MAKE UP ABOUT 80 PERCENT OF THE DRONE MARKET IN THE COMING YEARS.

DRONE DELIVERY!

Imagine ordering something online and watching it arrive from the sky! Big trucks that use a lot of **fossil fuels**, such as gasoline, usually deliver, or take, goods to those who ordered them. Burning this fuel makes climate change worse.

A California study found using small drones could save up to about 54 percent of the fuel used to deliver goods in that state. In 2013, the company Amazon showed how its drone delivery system could one day deliver some orders in just 30 minutes!

DRONE DETAILS

IN MAY 2019, A DRONE DELIVERED AN ORGAN FOR THE FIRST TIME. THE KIDNEY WAS CARRIED ON A 2.7 MILE (4.3 KM) FLIGHT TO A WOMAN IN MARYLAND. DRONE ORGAN DELIVERIES COULD SAVE THOUSANDS OF LIVES!

A drone in France demonstrates, or shows, what delivering packages by drone could look like.

STAYING SAFE UP THERE

There are many government regulations, or rules, involving drones to help keep people safe. An important one: Drones must stay away from airports and other locations, such as sporting events. Drone pilots can learn more about these locations by using a smartphone app called B4UFly.

Companies such as Amazon are working to find ways to make their plans for drone deliveries happen while following these rules. But some regulations, such as drone pilots keeping their drones in sight at all times, may need to be changed.

DRONE FLYING CHECKLIST

as of 2019

- ✓ DO NOT FLY OVER 400 FEET (122 M)
- ✓ KEEP THE DRONE IN SIGHT AT ALL TIMES
- ✓ STAY A SAFE DISTANCE AWAY FROM AIRPORTS AND AIRPLANES, WHICH ALWAYS HAVE THE RIGHT OF WAY
- ✓ AVOID FLYING OVER PEOPLE
- ✓ DON'T GET TOO CLOSE TO STADIUMS OR SPORTS EVENTS
- ✓ KEEP AWAY FROM EMERGENCY AREAS, OR AREAS WITH UNEXPECTED DANGERS
- ✓ DON'T FLY A DRONE IF DRINKING OR USING DRUGS
- ✓ USE THE B4UFLY APP TO KNOW WHERE YOU CAN'T FLY (CONTROLLED AIRSPACE)

TAKING GREEN TO NEW HEIGHTS

Drones are often made out of things that aren't good for the environment. Today, some people make drones out of parts that are biodegradable, or able to be broken down and become part of the soil. Drones made from cardboard can biodegrade in just a few months!

NASA has created some drone bodies partly from fungi, or small living things that look like plants and make their own food. These drones were also made with wasp spit! How else can these cool flying robots save the planet? You can help decide!

GLOSSARY

astrophysicist: A scientist who studies the properties and structures of stars, planets, and other objects in outer space.

environment: The natural world around us.

fertilizer: Things such as chemicals that are added to soil to help plants grow.

fossil fuel: A fuel—such as coal, oil, or natural gas—that is formed in the earth from dead plants or animals.

infrared: Used to describe light at the far red end of the spectrum that people cannot see and that gives off heat.

remote control: A small machine that is used to control another machine from a distance using electric signals.

satellite: A machine that is sent into space and circles the Earth, moon, or a planet.

solar panel: A large, flat machine that uses the sun's light to create electricity.

storm surge: The seawater level rise caused by a storm.

wind turbine: A tall structure that produces electricity from wind using large blades attached to an engine.

INDEX

A

Amazon, 18, 20

B

B4UFly, 20, 21
BioCarbon Engineering, 6, 7

C

climate change, 6, 8, 12, 16, 18

F

farming, 16, 17
Federal Aviation Administration, 4
forest fire, 4, 8, 9
fossil fuel, 18

N

NASA, 15, 22

P

Pennypacker, Carlton, 8

S

safety rules, 20

W

wildlife, 4, 10, 11
wind turbine, 14

Z

Zappa, Christopher, 12

WEBSITES

Due to the changing nature of Internet links, PowerKids Press has developed an online list of websites related to the subject of this book. This site is updated regularly. Please use this link to access the list: www.powerkidslinks.com/dae/environ